CW00514972

Table of Contents

Gluten Free Cakes!

The #1 All Gluten Free Cooking Recipes

Pamela James

Coconut Cupcakes With Key Lime Frosting

Prep Time: 10 mins

Total Time: 30 mins

Serves: 4-6, **Yield**: 10 cupcakes

Ingredients
- 3 eggs
- 1/2 cup coconut oil
- 1/2 cup agave nectar
- 1/2 cup coconut flour
- 1/2 teaspoon celtic sea salt
- 1/2 baking soda
- 1/2 cup shredded coconut

Directions
1. Preheat the oven to 350°F temperature.
2. Use hand mixer to combine the coconut oil, agave nectar and eggs in a small bowl.
3. Add the baking soda, salt and the coconut flour.
4. Let it sit thicken a little.
5. Line the unbleached baking cups on cupcake tins.

6. Fill the baking cups with about 1/4 cup batter.
7. Place in the oven then bake for about 20-25 minutes.
8. Let the cupcakes cool down for around 20 minutes.
9. Top with Key Lime Frosting then serve.

NUTRITION FACTS

Serving Size: 1 (23 g)
Servings Per Recipe: 8

Amount Per Serving	% Daily Value
Calories 93.1	
Calories from Fat 80	86%

Amount Per Serving	% Daily Value
Total Fat 8.9g	13%
Saturated Fat 1.4g	7%
Cholesterol 69.7mg	23%
Sugars 0.1 g	
Sodium 178.5mg	7%
Total Carbohydrate 1.6g	0%
Dietary Fiber 0.8g	3%
Sugars 0.1 g	0%
Protein 2.8g	5%

Gluten-Free Strawberry Shortcake

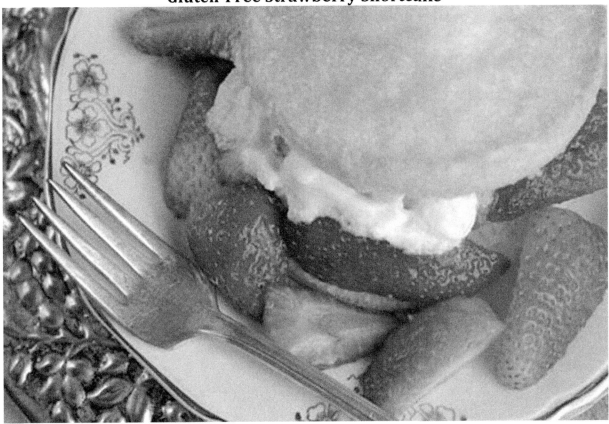

Prep Time: 15 mins

Total Time: 30 mins

Serves: 12-15, **Yield:** 12 Little cakes

Ingredients
- 1/2 cup butter
- 1 cup icing sugar
- 4 eggs
- 1 teaspoon vanilla
- 1 cup cornstarch
- 1 1/4 teaspoons baking powder

Directions
1. Preheat the oven to 375°F temperature.
2. Grease a 12-piece muffin pan.
3. Use an electric mixer to beat the sugar and cream butter in a large bowl.
4. Pour vanilla then add the eggs. Mix well until the mixture becomes light and fluffy.

5. Mix the baking powder and cornstarch using a small bowl. Slowly add the contents to the large bowl.

6. Quick tip: Do not add hastily to avoid mess in the kitchen.

7. Continue to mix until completely blended.

8. Fill the muffin pan with the mixture until half full.

9. Place into the preheated oven then bake for about 15 minutes.

10. Quick tip: After 15 minutes, test using a toothpick even when the top still looks shiny.

11. While still warm, remove the muffins from the pan. Best served whipped cream and strawberries.

NUTRITION FACTS

Serving Size: 1 (38 g)
Servings Per Recipe: 12

Amount Per Serving	% Daily Value
Calories 172.4	
Calories from Fat 83	48%

Amount Per Serving	% Daily Value
Total Fat 9.2g	14%
Saturated Fat 5.3g	26%
Cholesterol 82.3mg	27%
Sugars 9.8 g	
Sodium 130.2mg	5%
Total Carbohydrate 20.0g	6%
Dietary Fiber 0.1g	0%
Sugars 9.8 g	39%
Protein 2.2g	4%

Molten Lava Cakes - Gluten-Free

Prep Time: 3 mins

Total Time: 15 mins

Serves: 2-3, **Yield:** 3.0 cakes

Ingredients

- 2 tablespoons butter
- 1/3 cup sugar
- 2 ounces dark chocolate
- 1 large egg
- 1 egg yolk

- 1 pinch salt
- 3 tablespoons flour
- butter, for coating ramekins
- sugar, for coating ramekins

Directions

1. Preheat the oven to 400°F temperature.

2. Grease the ramekins with butter then sprinkle with sugar.

Quick tip: As an alternative to ramekins, a silicone muffin tray may be used.

2. Melt the butter and chocolate.

3. In a bowl, mix the eggs, salt and sugar.

4. Add the butter, sugar, and chocolate.

5. Add the flour then mix altogether until well blended. Make sure not to over whisk.

6. Fill the ramekins then place in the preheated oven. Bake for about 10-12 minutes.

Quick tip: Test the cake by inserting 1/2 of the toothpick on the ramekin's side. The cake is baked when the toothpick comes out clean.

7. Remove the ramekins from the oven. Allow to sit for at least 10 minutes.

8. Serving suggestions:

- Sprinkle with icing sugar
- Serve with ice cream
- Serve with your favorite berries

NUTRITION FACTS

Serving Size: 1 (80 g)
Servings Per Recipe: 2

Amount Per Serving	% Daily Value
Calories 475.7	
Calories from Fat 277	58%

Amount Per Serving	% Daily Value
Total Fat 30.8g	47%
Saturated Fat 18.0g	90%
Cholesterol 206.5mg	68%
Sugars 33.6 g	
Sodium 225.4mg	9%
Total Carbohydrate 51.1g	17%
Dietary Fiber 5.0g	20%
Sugars 33.6 g	134%
Protein 9.3g	18%

Orange and Almond Cake (Gluten-Free)

Prep Time: 2 hrs

Total Time: 3 hrs

Serves: 8, Yield: 1 cake

Ingredients

- 1 orange (large)
- 4 -5 eggs
- 200 g caster sugar
- 300 g almond meal
- 1 teaspoon baking powder
- caster sugar (for dusting)
- icing sugar (for dusting after baking)
- butter (or oil spray for greasing pan.)

Directions

1. In boiling water, put the unpeeled orange for about 2 hours. Drain the water then set aside.

2. Preheat the oven to 350°F temperature.

3. In a blender, put the eggs and caster sugar. Blend well.

4. Cut the unpeeled and boiled orange then add into the egg mixture. Blend until completely smooth.

5. Add the baking powder and the almond meal. Continue to blend well.

6. Use butter or oil spray to grease the baking pan then dust with caster sugar.

7. Pour the batter into the greased pan. Dust again with caster sugar on top.

8. Place into the preheated oven then bake until the top is golden brown, for about 1 hr.

9. Take out from oven then let it cool down.

10. To serve, dust with cream or icing sugar.

NUTRITION FACTS

Serving Size: 1 (119 g)
Servings Per Recipe: 8

Amount Per Serving	% Daily Value
Calories 356.1	
Calories from Fat 188	52%

Amount Per Serving	% Daily Value
Total Fat 20.9g	32%
Saturated Fat 2.1g	10%
Cholesterol 93.0mg	31%
Sugars 28.0 g	
Sodium 81.5mg	3%
Total Carbohydrate 35.3g	11%
Dietary Fiber 4.9g	19%
Sugars 28.0 g	112%
Protein 11.2g	22%

Gluten-Free Strawberry Cake

Prep Time: 10 mins

Total Time: 45 mins

Servings: 12

Ingredients
- 2 1/2 cups gluten-free flour
- 1 cup sugar
- 2/3 cup oil
- 4 eggs
- 1 (3 ounce) boxes strawberry gelatin
- 1 (16 ounce) containers frozen strawberries with sugar, thawed
- 1 tablespoon baking powder
- 1 teaspoon xanthan gum
- 1 teaspoon vanilla
- 1/2 teaspoon salt

Directions
1. Preheat the oven to 350°F temperature.

2. Grease 2 9-inch baking pans.

3. Combine the flour, sugar, oil, eggs, gelatin, thawed strawberries, baking powder, xanthan gum, vanilla and salt in a large bowl.

4. Use an electric mixer to mix the ingredients altogether with medium speed for about 2 minutes.

5. Pour the batter equally into the 2 greased pans.

6. Place the pans into the preheated oven then bake the cake for about 35 to 40 minutes. Alternatively, 20 minutes for cupcakes.

Quick tip: Test the cake by inserting 1/2 of the toothpick in the middle of the pan. The cake is baked when the toothpick comes out clean.

NUTRITION FACTS

Serving Size: 1 (54 g)
Servings Per Recipe: 12

Amount Per Serving	% Daily Value
Calories 224.0	
Calories from Fat 123	55%

Amount Per Serving	% Daily Value
Total Fat 13.7g	21%
Saturated Fat 2.0g	10%
Cholesterol 62.0mg	20%
Sugars 22.8 g	
Sodium 244.5mg	10%
Total Carbohydrate 23.5g	7%
Dietary Fiber 0.0g	0%
Sugars 22.8 g	91%
Protein 2.6g	5%

Blueberries and Cream Cupcakes

Prep Time: 10 mins

Total Time: 30 mins

Serves: 4-6, **Yield:** 9 cupcakes

Ingredients
- 1/2 cup coconut flour, sifted
- 1/4 teaspoon celtic sea salt
- 1/4 teaspoon baking soda
- 3 eggs
- 1/2 cup agave nectar
- 1/2 cup grapeseed oil
- 1 tablespoon vanilla extract
- 1 cup frozen blueberries (for cupcakes)
- fresh blueberries (for decorating)

Directions

1. Preheat the oven to 350°F temperature.

2. Combine the baking soda, coconut flour and salt in a small bowl.

3. Combine the eggs, grapeseed oil, vanilla, and agave in a large bowl. Use a hand mixer to blend the ingredients well.

4. Pour the contents of the small bowl into the large bowl, then mix well using the hand mixer.

5. Gradually add the frozen blueberries.

6. Use a 1/4 measuring cup to scoop the batter into paper-lined cupcake tins.

7. Place the cupcake tins into the preheated oven then bake for about 20-25 minutes.

8. Allow the cupcakes to cool for about 1-2 hours then frost with whipped cream.

9. Top the cupcakes with around 4-5 fresh blueberries before serving.

NUTRITION FACTS

Serving Size: 1 (95 g)
Servings Per Recipe: 4

Amount Per Serving	% Daily Value
Calories 351.9	
Calories from Fat 279	79%

Amount Per Serving	% Daily Value
Total Fat 31.0g	47%
Saturated Fat 3.7g	18%
Cholesterol 158.6mg	52%
Sugars 12.0 g	
Sodium 277.3mg	11%
Total Carbohydrate 13.3g	4%
Dietary Fiber 1.2g	5%
Sugars 12.0 g	48%
Protein 4.9g	9%

Pecan Apple Strudel Cake (Gluten-Free)

Prep Time: 40 mins

Total Time: 1 hr 40 mins

Serves: 6, **Yield**: 1 cake

Ingredients

Strudel
- 1 cup pecans, finely chopped or 1 cup blanched slivered almond, crushed
- 2 tablespoons brown rice flour
- 4 tablespoons brown sugar
- 1 tablespoon canola oil
- 1 teaspoon cinnamon

Cake Batter
- 1/3 cup chopped pecans or 1/3 cup blanched slivered almond, crushed
- 1/2 cup rice flour (white)

- 1/2 cup brown rice flour
- 1/3 cup tapioca starch
- 3/4 teaspoon guar gum (xanthan gum may be substituted ~ corn derived)
- 1 teaspoon baking soda
- 1 1/2 teaspoons gluten-free baking powder
- 1 teaspoon cinnamon
- 2 teaspoons vanilla
- 1/2 cup canola oil
- 3/4 cup dark brown sugar
- 2 egg replacer eggs
- 4 tablespoons orange juice
- 1 1/2 cups chopped apples (about 2 apples)

Directions

1. Preheat the oven to 325°F temperature.
2. Grease a deep small pan then dust with white rice flour.
3. In a small bowl, mix all the ingredients for the strudel then set aside.
4. Strain all the dry ingredients into a medium bowl.
5. Pour the wet ingredients into the medium bowl then mix using a wooden spoon.
6. Put in the chopped apples then stir well.
7. Pour half of the batter into the greased pan then layer with half of the strudel mixture.
8. Pour the remaining half of the batter and then the remaining strudel mixture on top.
9. Bake for about an hour.

Quick tip: Test the cake by inserting 1/2 of the toothpick in the middle of the pan. The cake is baked when the toothpick comes out clean.

10. Let the cake cool down for at least 10 minutes or at room temperature before serving.

NUTRITION FACTS		Amount Per Serving	% Daily Value
Serving Size: 1 (172 g)		Total Fat 40.2g	61%
Servings Per Recipe: 6		Saturated Fat 3.6g	18%
Amount Per Serving	% Daily Value	Cholesterol 62.0mg	20%
		Sugars 41.0 g	
Calories 646.6			
Calories from Fat 362	56%	Sodium 245.6mg	10%
		Total Carbohydrate 68.8g	22%
		Dietary Fiber 4.6g	18%
		Sugars 41.0 g	164%
		Protein 6.5g	13%

Gluten-Free Date Pecan Muffins

Prep Time: 13 mins

Total Time: 58 mins

Serves: 12, **Yield:** 12 muffins

Ingredients

- 3 cups blanched almond flour
- 1/2 teaspoon sea salt
- 1/2 teaspoon baking soda
- 1/4 teaspoon ground nutmeg
- 1/4 cup grapeseed oil (canola oil can be used)

- 2 tablespoons agave nectar
- 2 large eggs
- 1 tablespoon vanilla extract
- 2 medium apples, peeled, cored and sliced
- 1 cup pecans, coarsely chopped
- 1/2 cup dates, chopped into 1/4-inch pieces

Directions

1. Preheat the oven to 350°F temperature.

2. Use paper liners to line 12 muffin tin cups.

3. Whisk the almond flour, nutmeg, baking soda and flour into a large bowl.

4. Use a blender to combine the apples, vanilla, eggs, agave nectar and grapeseed oil over high speed.

5. Pour all the wet ingredients into the large bowl of flour mixture then stir well. Add the dates and pecans.

6. Scoop batter into the lined muffin cups.

7. Place in the preheated oven then bake until the top of the muffins become golden brown for about 35-45 minutes.

Quick tip: Test the cake by inserting 1/2 of the toothpick in the middle of the pan. The cake is baked when the toothpick comes out clean.

8. Allow the muffins cool for about for 30 minutes while in the pan then serve.

NUTRITION FACTS

Serving Size: 1 (60 g)
Servings Per Recipe: 12

Amount Per Serving	% Daily Value
Calories 151.4	
Calories from Fat 107	71%

Amount Per Serving	% Daily Value
Total Fat 11.9g	18%
Saturated Fat 1.2g	6%
Cholesterol 35.2mg	11%
Sugars 7.6 g	
Sodium 161.4mg	6%
Total Carbohydrate 10.2g	3%
Dietary Fiber 2.0g	8%
Sugars 7.6 g	30%
Protein 2.1g	4%

Gluten-Free Twinkies

Prep Time: 20 mins

Total Time: 35 mins

Serves: 4-8, **Yield**: 8 twinkies

Ingredients
- 3 eggs, separated
- 1/4 cup grapeseed oil
- 1/4 cup agave nectar
- 1 tablespoon vanilla extract
- 1 tablespoon lemon juice
- 6 tablespoons coconut flour
- 1/2 teaspoon baking soda
- 1/4 teaspoon celtic sea salt
- 2 egg whites
- 1/4 cup agave nectar

Directions

For the Twinkie
1. Preheat the oven 350°F temperature.

2. Beat the egg whites in a large bowl until the peaks stiff. Set aside.

3. Beat the egg yolks in a medium bowl until it becomes pale yellow.

4. Pour the agave and grapeseed oil then whip again.

5. Add and whip the lemon juice and vanilla then continue to whip.

6. In a separate medium bowl, combine the baking soda, coconut flour and salt then pour into the egg yolk mixture.

7. Whip all the ingredients until completely smooth. Fold in the egg whites.

8. Place in the preheated oven then bake for about 11-12 minutes.

9. Take out from the oven then let the Twinkies cool down.

For the Filling

1. Beat the egg whites until the peaks stiff.

2. Pour the agave then whip until the peaks stiff again.

3. Pour the filling into the filling injector.

4. Lay the Twinkie with flat side up. Inject the filling into the Twinkie then serve.

NUTRITION FACTS

Serving Size: 1 (37 g)
Servings Per Recipe: 4

Amount Per Serving	% Daily Value
Calories 194.4	
Calories from Fat 156	80%

Amount Per Serving	% Daily Value
Total Fat 17.3g	26%
Saturated Fat 2.4g	12%
Cholesterol 158.6mg	52%
Sugars 0.9 g	
Sodium 382.8mg	15%
Total Carbohydrate 1.1g	0%
Dietary Fiber 0.0g	0%
Sugars 0.9 g	3%
Protein 6.5g	13%

Gluten-Free Apple and Sour Cherry Cake

Prep Time: 10 mins

Total Time: 50 mins

Serves: 6, Yield: 1 cake

Ingredients
- 4 apples
- 6 eggs
- 1 teaspoon finely grated lemon zest
- 2 cups caster sugar
- 2 cups gluten-free self-raising flour
- 1 teaspoon vegetable oil
- 200 g morello pitted cherries, drained
- cinnamon sugar

Directions
1. Preheat the oven to 350°F temperature.

2. Use baking paper to line a 22cm cake tin.

3. Peel and cut the apples into thin slices.

4. Beat the eggs, sugar and lemon zest for about 8 minutes, or until the mixture becomes creamy and thick.

5. Gently pour the flour into the mixture. Whip until the batter's consistency is similar to sour cream.

6. Pour the vegetable oil into the pan.

7. Lay the cherries and apples at the bottom then pour the batter consistently over.

8. Place the pan into the preheated oven until the top becomes golden brown for about 40 minutes.

9. Allow the cake to cool down for at least 5 minutes then turn it upside down to a tray or plate.

10. Top with cinnamon sugar then serve with whipped cream.

NUTRITION FACTS

Serving Size: 1 (272 g)
Servings Per Recipe: 6

Amount Per Serving	% Daily Value
Calories 420.3	
Calories from Fat 52	12%

Amount Per Serving	% Daily Value
Total Fat 5.7g	8%
Saturated Fat 1.7g	8%
Cholesterol 186.0mg	62%
Sugars 83.6 g	
Sodium 72.9mg	3%
Total Carbohydrate 89.1g	29%
Dietary Fiber 3.6g	14%
Sugars 83.6 g	334%
Protein 6.9g	13%

Prep Time: 20 mins

Total Time: 1 hr 10 mins

Serves: 12, Yield: 1 Cake

Ingredients

- 3 eggs
- 1 1/2 cups sugar
- 1 cup sunflower oil
- 2 teaspoons vanilla
- 2 cups carrots, shredded
- 10 ounces crushed pineapple in juice
- 1 cup shredded coconut
- 1 cup raisins, soaked in tea, drained
- 1 cup walnuts, chopped
- 2 cups white corn flour

- 4 teaspoons baking soda
- 1 teaspoon salt
- 1/4 teaspoon cinnamon
- 1/8 teaspoon nutmeg
- 1 tablespoon xanthan gum

Directions

1. Preheat the oven to 350∘F temperature.
2. Whip the sugar and eggs in a large bowl into it mixture becomes pale yellow.
3. Pour the vanilla and sunflower oil then continue beating.
4. Add the walnuts, raisins, coconut, pineapple and shredded carrots. Mix well.
5. Whisk the xanthan gum, nutmeg, cinnamon, salt, baking soda and corn flour into a separate bowl.
6. Combine the dry ingredients into the egg mixture then mix well.
7. Pour the batter into a 9x11 or large bundt pan.
8. Place the pan into the preheated oven then bake for about 50 minutes.
Quick tip: Test the cake by inserting 1/2 of the toothpick in the middle of the pan. The cake is baked when the toothpick comes out clean.
9. Allow the cake to cool completely then top with cream cheese icing.

NUTRITION FACTS

Serving Size: 1 (152 g)
Servings Per Recipe: 12

Amount Per Serving	% Daily Value
Calories 509.5	
Calories from Fat 264	51%

Amount Per Serving	% Daily Value
Total Fat 29.3g	45%
Saturated Fat 5.9g	29%
Cholesterol 46.5mg	15%
Sugars 40.4 g	
Sodium 669.1mg	27%
Total Carbohydrate 60.5g	20%
Dietary Fiber 3.6g	14%
Sugars 40.4 g	161%
Protein 5.3g	10%

Gluten-Free Pumpkin-Applesauce Bundt Cake

Prep Time: 15 mins

Total Time: 1 hr 15 mins

Serves: 12-16, **Yield:** 14 slices

Ingredients

- 2 cups sugar
- 2 cups pumpkin
- 1 cup applesauce
- 1/2 cup canola oil
- 4 eggs
- 2 cups gluten-free rice flour mix
- 1 teaspoon salt
- 1 teaspoon baking soda
- 2 teaspoons baking powder
- 2 teaspoons cinnamon

Directions

1. Preheat the oven to 350°F temperature.
2. Grease a large bundt pan.
3. In a large bowl, whip the eggs until fluffy.
4. Mix by hand or a mixer on low the oil, applesauce, pumpkin and sugar. Be careful not to overmix.
5. Put in all the dry ingredients while blending one at a time together.
6. Pour the batter into the greased pan.
7. Place the pan into the preheated oven then bake for about an hour.
Quick tip: Test the cake by inserting 1/2 of the toothpick in the middle of the pan. The cake is baked when the toothpick comes out clean.

NUTRITION FACTS

Serving Size: 1 (76 g)
Servings Per Recipe: 12

Amount Per Serving	% Daily Value
Calories 255.7	
Calories from Fat 96	37%

Amount Per Serving	% Daily Value
Total Fat 10.7g	16%
Saturated Fat 1.2g	6%
Cholesterol 62.0mg	20%
Sugars 33.6 g	
Sodium 389.3mg	16%
Total Carbohydrate 39.4g	13%
Dietary Fiber 0.5g	2%
Sugars 33.6 g	134%
Protein 2.3g	4%

Gluten-Free Sour Cream Coffee Cake

Prep Time: 40 mins

Total Time: 1 hr 25 mins

Serves: 12-16, **Yield:** 1 coffee cake

Ingredients
- 2/3 cup chopped pecans
- 2 1/2 tablespoons brown sugar
- 2 teaspoons ground cinnamon

Batter
- 1 cup butter, softened
- 2 cups sugar
- 2 eggs
- 1 teaspoon vanilla extract
- 2 cups gluten-free baking mix
- 1 1/2 teaspoons xanthan gum

- 1 1/2 teaspoons baking powder
- 1/4 teaspoon baking soda
- 1/4 teaspoon salt
- 1 cup sour cream
- confectioners' sugar, for dusting

Directions

1. Preheat the oven to 350°F temperature.

2. Grease a 10-inch bundt pan then sprinkle with flour.

3. Put in and mix the cinnamon, brown sugar and pecans in a small bowl then set aside.

4. Whip the sugar and butter into a large bowl until it becomes light and fluffy.

5. Put in and beat the eggs one at a time.

6. Pour and whip the vanilla.

7. Mix the salt, baking soda, baking powder and the flour in a separate bowl. Pour the contents, alternatively with the sour cream, on the sugar and butter mixture.

8. Pour the first half of the batter the greased pan.

9. Top with the first half of the pecan and cinnamon mixture.

10. Pour the remaining half of the batter then the pecan mixture next.

11. Place the pan into the preheated oven then bake for about 45-50 minutes.

Quick tip: Test the cake by inserting 1/2 of the toothpick in the middle of the pan. The cake is baked when the toothpick comes out clean.

12. Allow the cake to cool for about 10 minutes. Remove from the pan then move to a wire rack.

13. Let it cool down completely then sprinkle with confectioner's sugar.

NUTRITION FACTS

Serving Size: 1 (83 g)
Servings Per Recipe: 12

Amount Per Serving	% Daily Value
Calories 460.0	
Calories from Fat 248	53%

Amount Per Serving	% Daily Value
Total Fat 27.5g	42%
Saturated Fat 13.4g	67%
Cholesterol 82.0mg	27%
Sugars 39.5 g	
Sodium 499.3mg	20%
Total Carbohydrate 51.6g	17%
Dietary Fiber 1.2g	5%
Sugars 39.5 g	158%
Protein 3.8g	7%

Easy Gluten-Free Red Velvet Cupcakes

Prep Time: 20 mins

Total Time: 40 mins

Serves: 12, **Yield:** 24 cupcakes

Ingredients

- 1 (15 ounce) boxes betty crocker gluten-free yellow cake mix
- 1 (3 1/2 ounce) packages chocolate-flavored instant pudding mix (Jello brand is gluten-free) or 1 (3 1/2 ounce) packages pie filling (Jello brand is gluten-free)
- 1/2 cup butter, softened (no substitutes!)
- 8 ounces sour cream
- 3 eggs
- 2/3 cup milk
- 2 tablespoons red food coloring (McCormick's and Tones are gluten-free)
- 8 ounces cold cream cheese (Philadelphia is gluten-free)
- 5 tablespoons softened butter
- 2 teaspoons pure vanilla extract
- 3 cups powdered sugar
- 1 pinch salt

Directions

For the cupcakes
1. Preheat the oven to 350°F temperature.
2. In a large bowl, use a hand mixer to mix the pudding mix, yellow cake mix, butter, sour cream, eggs, milk and food coloring over medium speed for about 2 minutes or until smooth.
3. Line the muffin pans with cupcake liners.
4. Scoop the mixture into the muffin pans.
5. Place the muffin pans into the preheated oven then bake for about 16-20 minutes.
Quick tip: Test the cake by inserting 1/2 of the toothpick in the middle of the pan. The cake is baked when the toothpick comes out clean.
6. Allow the cupcakes to cool while still in the pans. After 5 minutes, take the cupcakes out then move to the cooling racks.
7. Let the cupcakes cool in the pans for five minutes, then carefully remove them and place them on cooling racks.

For the Frosting
1. Mix the vanilla, butter and cream cheese then add the salt.
2. With the mixer on slow, gently pour the powdered sugar. Taste to check
Quick tip: Refrigerate the cupcakes when not eaten within 12-24 hours.

NUTRITION FACTS

Serving Size: 1 (154 g)
Servings Per Recipe: 12

Amount Per Serving	% Daily Value
Calories 543.2	
Calories from Fat 258	47%

Amount Per Serving	% Daily Value
Total Fat 28.7g	44%
Saturated Fat 15.2g	76%
Cholesterol 113.3mg	37%
Sugars 53.8 g	
Sodium 576.8mg	24%
Total Carbohydrate 67.5g	22%
Dietary Fiber 0.3g	1%
Sugars 53.8 g	215%
Protein 5.2g	10%

Easy Madeleines With Gluten-Free Option

Prep Time: 20 mins

Total Time: 40 mins

Serves: 4, **Yield:** 8 Madeleines

Ingredients

- 210 g unsalted butter
- 1/2 cup plain flour or 1/2 cup blended gluten-free plain flour
- 1 2/3 cups icing sugar (confectioner's sugar)
- 1/2 cup ground almonds (almond meal)
- 6 large egg whites
- 1 tablespoon honey

Directions

1. Preheat the oven to 350°F temperature.
2. Over medium heat, melt the butter in a saucepan.

3. Brush a little butter on the Madeleine mould then sprinkle with gluten-free flour. Set aside after shaking off the extra flour.

4. Let the butter cook until it turns golden brown for about 5 minutes. Do not overcook the butter.

5. Remove from heat then pour into a ceramic bowl. Set aside.

6. In a medium bowl, sieve the flour and the icing sugar. Add the almond meal or ground almonds.

7. Use another bowl to beat the egg whites until fluffy. Combine with the almond mixture then whisk the honey and butter.

8. Fill the buttered moulds with the batter.

9. Place into the preheated oven then bake until the Madeleines are springy to touch with light golden appearance, for about 12-15 minutes.

Note: Madeleines may appear very light in color if using gluten-free flour.

10. Take out from the oven then let it cool. After 10 minutes, tap on the hard surface to remove the Madeleines from the mould.

11. Serve with fresh strawberries or whipped cream, or simply sprinkle with icing sugar, or dip in melted chocolate.

NUTRITION FACTS

Serving Size: 1 (184 g)
Servings Per Recipe: 4

Amount Per Serving	% Daily Value
Calories 737.8	
Calories from Fat 438	59%

Amount Per Serving	% Daily Value
Total Fat 48.6g	74%
Saturated Fat 27.4g	137%
Cholesterol 112.8mg	37%
Sugars 54.1 g	
Sodium 89.5mg	3%
Total Carbohydrate 69.1g	23%
Dietary Fiber 1.8g	7%
Sugars 54.1 g	216%
Protein 9.9g	19%

Vanilla Sponge Cake- Gluten, Dairy, Nut and Egg Free

Prep Time: 20 mins

Total Time: 1 hr 20 mins

Serves: 10, Yield: 1 cake

Ingredients

- 1 1/2 cups plain flour (use a typical blended general purpose gluten-free plain flour mix -as stated in the intro)
- 1 cup sugar
- 1/3 cup oil (I use vegetable oil)
- 1 cup water
- 1 teaspoon gluten-free baking powder
- 1 teaspoon gluten-free bicarbonate of soda
- 1 teaspoon vanilla
- 1 tablespoon vinegar or 1 tablespoon orange juice

Directions

1. Preheat oven to 350°F temperature.

2. Grease an 8-inch/20cm pan for the cake or cupcake tins for cupcakes, then line with paper liner.

3. In a large bowl, whisk the flour, sugar and baking powder.

4. Mix well the water, vanilla, vinegar and oil in a mixing jug.

5. Form a well at the center of the flour mix then pour the wet mixture over. Use a wooden spoon to gradually beat altogether for about 2 minutes.

6. Fill the pan or cupcakes tins with the batter.

7. Place in the preheated oven then bake for about 45-60 minutes.

8. Take out the pan from the oven then allow let it cool down. After about 5-10 minutes, remove the cake or cupcakes then serve with frosting and favorite fruit.

NUTRITION FACTS

Serving Size: 1 (71 g)
Servings Per Recipe: 10

Amount Per Serving	% Daily Value
Calories 211.3	
Calories from Fat 66	31%

Amount Per Serving	% Daily Value
Total Fat 7.4g	11%
Saturated Fat 0.9g	4%
Cholesterol 0.0mg	0%
Sugars 20.0 g	
Sodium 1.3mg	0%
Total Carbohydrate 34.3g	11%
Dietary Fiber 0.5g	2%
Sugars 20.0 g	80%
Protein 1.9g	3%

Gluten-Free Moist Mango and Nut Bread

Prep Time: 15 mins

Total Time: 1 hr 15 mins

Serves: 6-8, **Yield:** 2 small loaves

Ingredients

- 1 cup gluten-free all-purpose baking flour (you can substitute with all purpose baking flour for a regular recipe, and if you can tolerate glute)
- 3 teaspoons baking powder
- 1/2 cup brown sugar
- 2 teaspoons coconut oil
- 1/4 teaspoon salt
- 2 large eggs
- 1/2 cup macadamia nuts or 1/2 cup walnuts, chopped
- 300 g raw mangoes, pureed or 2 -3 mangoes, depending on the size
- 2 teaspoons vanilla extract

- 1 teaspoon cinnamon (optional)

Directions
1. Preheat the oven to 350°F temperature.
2. Grease 2 small cake or loaf pans.
3. Whisk the flour, salt, cinnamon (if desired) and baking powder in a large bowl.
4. Separate the egg whites and egg yolks into 2 separate bowls.
5. Use a hand mixer or electric beater to stiffen the egg whites.
6. Do the same with the egg yolks, but adding the sugar, vanilla and oil.
7. Pour and mix the egg yolk mixture into the flour mixture.
8. Fold in the egg whites until smooth.
9 Add the nuts and mangoes then mix well.
10. Pour the batter into the cake or loaf pans.

Quick tip: Test the cake by inserting 1/2 of the toothpick in the middle of the pan. The cake is baked when the toothpick comes out clean.

NUTRITION FACTS

Serving Size: 1 (100 g)
Servings Per Recipe: 6

Amount Per Serving	% Daily Value
Calories 240.5	
Calories from Fat 106	44%

Amount Per Serving	% Daily Value
Total Fat 11.8g	18%
Saturated Fat 3.2g	16%
Cholesterol 62.0mg	20%
Sugars 29.6 g	
Sodium 308.7mg	12%
Total Carbohydrate 32.5g	10%
Dietary Fiber 2.2g	9%
Sugars 29.6 g	118%
Protein 3.6g	7%

Gluten-Free Coconut Carrot Cake With Cream Cheese Icing

Prep Time: 25 mins

Total Time: 1 hr 5 mins

Serves: 8-10

Ingredients

Carrot Cake
- 3 large eggs, organic free-range

- 1/2 cup vegetable oil
- 1 cup light brown sugar, packed
- 1/3 cup plain yogurt
- 2 teaspoons vanilla extract
- 1/2 teaspoon ground cinnamon
- 1/2 teaspoon pumpkin pie spice (or a mix of nutmeg, cloves, ginger and allspice)
- 2 cups ultimate baking and pancake mix
- 3/4 cup sweetened flaked coconut
- 1 1/2 cups carrots, shredded (about 4)
- 1/2 cup golden raisin
- 1/2 pecans, toasted & chopped (or walnuts)

Cream Cheese Icing

- 4 ounces cream cheese, softened
- 2 tablespoons butter, softened
- 1 -2 teaspoon vanilla extract
- 3 cups powdered sugar (more, if needed)
- 1 teaspoon lemon juice (lime or orange)

Directions

For the cake

1. Preheat the oven to 350◦F temperature.
2. Grease a 9-inch spring-form cake pan.
3. Beat the eggs in a bowl. Pour the oil then beat. Pour the brown sugar then beat again until the mixture becomes smooth.
4. Pour the cinnamon, vanilla, yogurt and pumpkin pie spice then beat again.
5. Pour the baking mix then beat until completely combined.
Note: The batter should be a little thicker than the regular wheat flour batter.
6. Stir in the nuts, raisins, carrots and coconut using a wooden spoon.
7. Evenly pour the batter into the cake pan.
8. Place the pan in the center of the preheated oven then bake for about 40-45 minutes or until the cake is firm.
9. Let it cool then top with cream cheese frosting.

For the frosting

1. Beat the butter and cream cheese until fluffy.
2. Pour the vanilla.
3. Add a cup of powdered sugar at a time.
4. Pour a bit of orange or lemon juice into the mixture then continue to beat until smooth.
5. Add more juice or sugar, if desired.
6. Top on cooled cake.

NUTRITION FACTS

Serving Size: 1 (141 g)
Servings Per Recipe: 8

Amount Per Serving	% Daily Value
Calories 594.6	
Calories from Fat 241	40%

Amount Per Serving	% Daily Value
Total Fat 26.8g	41%
Saturated Fat 9.9g	49%
Cholesterol 94.3mg	31%
Sugars 82.2 g	
Sodium 151.5mg	6%
Total Carbohydrate 87.2g	29%
Dietary Fiber 1.5g	6%
Sugars 82.2 g	328%
Protein 4.4g	8%

Prep Time: 20 mins

Total Time: 1 hr 15 mins

Serves: 12, **Yield**: 1 cake

Ingredients

- 2 tablespoons canola oil
- 1 tablespoon honey (or agave nectar)
- 2 oranges, juice of
- 1 tablespoon Ener-G Egg Substitute, whisked with
- 1/4 cup warm water
- 1 tablespoon pure vanilla extract
- 1/2 cup sorghum flour
- 1/4 cup coconut flour
- 1/4 cup potato starch (do <u>not</u> use potato flour)
- 1/2 cup arrowroot
- 1/2 cup sugar

- 3 (1 g) packets stevia
- 1/4 teaspoon sea salt
- 1 pinch nutmeg
- 1 teaspoon baking powder
- 1/2 teaspoon baking soda
- 1 teaspoon guar gum
- 1 orange, zest of
- 1/4 cup shortening
- 1 tablespoon Southern Comfort
- 1/2 orange, zest of
- 3 drops natural yellow food coloring (optional)
- 2 drops natural red food coloring (optional)
- 2 cups powdered sugar
- 2 -3 tablespoons orange juice (as needed)
- orange sprinkles or sugar

Directions

1. Preheat the oven to 350°F temperature.
2. Use paper liners to line 12-cupcake or muffin pan.
3. Beat well the Egg substitute, vanilla, orange juice, honey and oil using an electric beater.
4. Add all the remaining ingredients then beat for about 2 minutes over medium speed.
5. Pour the batter into the muffin or cupcake pan.
6. Place the pan into the preheated oven then bake until slightly tender for about 20-25 minutes.
7. Take out the pan from the oven then let it cool for about 10 minutes. Remove the cupcakes from the pan then allow to cool on a wire rack.

For the frosting

1. Beat the orange zest, Southern Comfort, food color and shortening over medium high speed until smooth.
2. Sieve the sugar until completely blended then add the orange juice if necessary.
3. Frost into cupcakes then dust desired decorations.

NUTRITION FACTS

Serving Size: 1 (75 g)
Servings Per Recipe: 12

Amount Per Serving	% Daily Value
Calories 237.2	
Calories from Fat 61	25%

Amount Per Serving	% Daily Value
Total Fat 6.8g	10%
Saturated Fat 1.2g	6%
Cholesterol 0.0mg	0%
Sugars 31.0 g	
Sodium 134.2mg	5%
Total Carbohydrate 43.0g	14%
Dietary Fiber 0.7g	3%
Sugars 31.0 g	124%
Protein 0.7g	1%

Yummy Fudgy Mud Cake

Prep Time: 15 mins

Total Time: 1 hr 15 mins

Serves: 12

Ingredients

- 35 g cocoa powder
- 1/3 cup hot water
- 150 g dark chocolate
- 150 g unsalted butter
- 265 g brown sugar
- 1 cup ground almonds
- 4 eggs

Directions

1. Grease a 19cm square cake pan then line with paper liners.
2. Mix the hot water and cocoa powder in a large bowl until smooth.

3. Stir in the almonds, sugar, melted butter and chocolate.

4. Separate the egg yolks from the egg whites in separate bowls.

5. One at a time, pour the egg yolks into the large bowl.

6. Beat the egg whites until the peaks are soft.

7. Fold in the egg whites into the large bowl.

8. Pour the mixture into the cake pan.

9. Bake in an oven for about 1 hour and 15 minutes.

10. Take out from the oven then let it cool down.

11. Slice the cake into small squares then sprinkle with icing sugar.

NUTRITION FACTS

Serving Size: 1 (81 g)
Servings Per Recipe: 12

Amount Per Serving	% Daily Value
Calories 322.6	
Calories from Fat 214	66%

Amount Per Serving	% Daily Value
Total Fat 23.8g	36%
Saturated Fat 12.1g	60%
Cholesterol 97.3mg	32%
Sugars 21.9 g	
Sodium 37.6mg	1%
Total Carbohydrate 29.1g	9%
Dietary Fiber 4.3g	17%
Sugars 21.9 g	87%
Protein 6.3g	12%

Lemon Ricotta-Almond Cake (Gluten-Free)

Prep Time: 10 mins

Total Time: 40 mins

Serves: 12

Ingredients

- 3 eggs
- 1/2 cup almond meal or 1/2 cup almond flour
- 1/2 cup ricotta cheese
- 1/3 cup butter, melted
- 3/4 cup ultimate baking and pancake mix
- 7/8 cup sugar
- 1/2 teaspoon lemon extract
- 1 lemon, juice of
- 1/2 teaspoon lemon zest

Directions

1. Preheat the oven to 350°F temperature.
2. Grease an 8-inch round cake pan.
3. Beat sugar and eggs. Put in butter and almond meal. Stir well to combine.
4. Use a blender to beat the ricotta cheese or mash using hands. Put into the batter.
5. Mix thoroughly then pour the pancake mix.
6. Pour the batter with lemon extract, lemon juice and lemon zest then mix well.
7. Pour the batter into the greased cake pan then bake for about 30 minutes.
8. Let the cake cool for about 10 minutes.
9. Sprinkle with powdered sugar or with your favorite fruit. Serve warm.

NUTRITION FACTS

Serving Size: 1 (51 g)
Servings Per Recipe: 12

Amount Per Serving	% Daily Value
Calories 161.4	
Calories from Fat 86	53%

Amount Per Serving	% Daily Value
Total Fat 9.5g	14%
Saturated Fat 4.6g	23%
Cholesterol 65.2mg	21%
Sugars 14.8 g	
Sodium 71.5mg	2%
Total Carbohydrate 16.1g	5%
Dietary Fiber 0.5g	2%
Sugars 14.8 g	59%
Protein 3.6g	7%

Almond Chocolate Cake (No Flour)

Prep Time: 30 mins

Total Time: 1 hr 18 mins

Serves: 12

Ingredients

- 6 eggs, separated
- 2 1/2 cups blanched almonds, toasted
- 2 tablespoons sugar
- 1 1/4 cups sugar
- 1/2 cup butter, softened
- 3 ounces semisweet chocolate, grated
- 1/4 cup brewed espresso, cold
- 2 tablespoons baking cocoa
- 2 tablespoons orange juice
- 1 tablespoon instant espresso granules
- 1 teaspoon vanilla extract

- confectioners' sugar (optional)
- chocolate curls (optional)
- coffee beans (optional)

Directions

1. Preheat the oven to 350°F temperature.

2. Grease a 9-inch spring form cake pan.

3. Separate the egg yolks from egg whites. Set aside the egg yolks.

4. Put the egg whites into a small bowl then set aside for 30 minutes at room temperature.

5. In another small bowl, mix 2 tablespoons sugar and almonds.

6. In a food processor, pour small amounts of the almonds mixture. Cover then process fine textured. Set aside.

7. In a large bowl, beat the rest of the sugar and butter until creamy.

8. Put in one egg yolk at a time, beating in between.

9. Beat in the reserved almond mixture, vanilla, espresso granules, orange juice, cocoa, espresso and chocolate.

10. Beat the reserved egg whites on high speed until peak stiff forms.

11. Add the egg whites in the large bowl of batter.

12. Pour the batter into the greased pan then place on the baking sheet.

13. Place into the preheated oven then bake for about 42-48 minutes.

14. Take out from the oven then let it cool for 10 minutes on a wire rack.

15. Run a spatula on the edges of the pan to loosen the cake then allow to completely cool down.

16. To serve, sprinkle with coffee beans, chocolate curls or confectioners' sugar, if preferred.

NUTRITION FACTS

Serving Size: 1 (106 g)
Servings Per Recipe: 12

Amount Per Serving	% Daily Value
Calories 411.1	
Calories from Fat 268	65%

Amount Per Serving	% Daily Value
Total Fat 29.8g	45%
Saturated Fat 9.2g	46%
Cholesterol 113.3mg	37%
Sugars 24.7 g	
Sodium 111.6mg	4%
Total Carbohydrate 31.7g	10%
Dietary Fiber 4.5g	18%
Sugars 24.7 g	98%
Protein 10.8g	21%

Vanilla Cinnamon 'Mochi Cakes'

Prep Time: 5 mins

Total Time: 15 mins

Serves: 6, **Yield:** 12 cakes

Ingredients

- 1 cup sweet rice flour
- 1/2 teaspoon baking powder
- 1/2 teaspoon salt
- 1 egg, beaten
- 3 tablespoons sugar
- 1/4 teaspoon vanilla extract
- 1/2 cup water
- 1/4 teaspoon cinnamon

Directions

1. Preheat the oven to 375°F temperature.

2. Use coconut oil to grease the mini muffin pan.

3. In a large bowl, mix the flour, salt, cinnamon, sugar and baking powder.

4. In a small bowl, pour the water, vanilla and beaten egg then mix thoroughly.

5. Pour the egg mixture into the flour mixture then mix using a fork.

6. Pour the batter into the muffin pan.

7. Place the muffin pan into the preheated oven then bake for about 8 minutes.

8. Once the tops start cracking, bake for another 2 minutes.

9. Let it cool completely. Serve with icing or warm jelly.

NUTRITION FACTS

Serving Size: 1 (61 g)
Servings Per Recipe: 6

Amount Per Serving	% Daily Value
Calories 133.6	
Calories from Fat 10	87%

Amount Per Serving	% Daily Value
Total Fat 1.1g	1%
Saturated Fat 0.3g	1%
Cholesterol 31.0mg	10%
Sugars 6.3 g	
Sodium 236.5mg	9%
Total Carbohydrate 27.6g	9%
Dietary Fiber 0.6g	2%
Sugars 6.3 g	25%
Protein 2.6g	5%

Tasty Sugar Topped Gluten-Free Muffins

Prep Time: 15 mins

Total Time: 40 mins

Serves: 12, **Yield:** 12 muffins

Ingredients

- 12 ounces self raising wheat gluten-free flour
- 1 pinch salt
- 1 teaspoon baking powder
- 6 ounces caster sugar
- 6 ounces butter
- 1/2 cup apple puree
- 1 tablespoon white vinegar
- milk, to mix

Directions

1. Preheat the oven to 375°F temperature.
2. In a large bowl, mix the flour, salt, baking powder and butter.

3. Pour the apple puree, white vinegar and a bit of milk. Mix well.

4. Line the muffin tins with paper liners.

5. Fill the lined muffin tins with the batter.

6. Top a bit of sugar then place inside the preheated oven.

7. Bake the muffins for about 20-25 minutes. If using a loaf tin, bake for about 50 minutes.

NUTRITION FACTS

Serving Size: 1 (30 g)
Servings Per Recipe: 12

Amount Per Serving	% Daily Value
Calories 156.9	
Calories from Fat 103	65%

Amount Per Serving	% Daily Value
Total Fat 11.5g	17%
Saturated Fat 7.2g	36%
Cholesterol 30.4mg	10%
Sugars 14.1 g	
Sodium 124.8mg	5%
Total Carbohydrate 14.2g	4%
Dietary Fiber 0.0g	0%
Sugars 14.1 g	56%
Protein 0.1g	0%

Chocolate Hazelnut Friands

Prep Time: 15 mins

Total Time: 35 mins

Serves: 9, **Yield:** 9 friands

Ingredients
- 1/2 cup gluten-free flour (plain)
- 1/4 cup cocoa powder
- 1 1/3 cups icing sugar (gluten-free plus extra to dust)
- 1 1/4 cups hazelnut meal (ground hazelnuts)
- 80 g chocolate (dark eating finely chopped)
- 240 g unsalted butter (melted cooled)
- 6 egg whites (lightly beaten)

Directions
1. Preheat the oven to 350◦F temperature.
2. Slightly grease a 9 pieces of 1/2 cup friend pans.

3. In a medium-sized bowl, sieve the icing sugar and cocoa powder. Pour the chocolate and hazelnut meal then mix well.

4. Form a well at the center.

5. Put the egg whites and butter then mix completely.

6. Fill the greased pans with the batter.

Quick tip: Test a friand by inserting a toothpick. The friand is baked when the toothpick comes out clean.

7. Let the friand pans cool for about 5 minutes before transferring to a wire rack.

8. Sprinkle with icing sugar then serve.

NUTRITION FACTS

Serving Size: 1 (77 g)
Servings Per Recipe: 9

Amount Per Serving	% Daily Value
Calories 321.7	
Calories from Fat 239	74%

Amount Per Serving	% Daily Value
Total Fat 26.6g	40%
Saturated Fat 16.7g	83%
Cholesterol 57.3mg	19%
Sugars 17.6 g	
Sodium 42.4mg	1%
Total Carbohydrate 21.9g	7%
Dietary Fiber 2.2g	9%
Sugars 17.6 g	70%
Protein 4.2g	8%

Polenta Ricotta Cake

Prep Time: 20 mins

Total Time: 1 hr 10 mins

Serves: 8

Ingredients

- 1/2 cup currants
- 1/2 cup sultana
- 1/2 cup Madeira wine
- 250 g fresh ricotta cheese
- 3/4 cup sugar
- 1 1/2 cups polenta
- 1/2 cup orange juice
- 1/2 cup milk
- 1 grated orange, rind of

Directions

1. Preheat the oven to 350°F temperature.

2. Grease a 22cm spring form cake pan with butter.

3. Use a baking paper to line the cake pan.

4. Soak the sultanas and currants in Madeira wine for about 15 minutes.

5. In a large bowl, combine the orange juice, rind, milk, polenta, sugar and ricotta.

6. Pour the Madeira wine and soaked sultanas and currants then mix well using a wooden spoon.

7. Pour the batter into the greased pan.

8. Place the pan into the preheated oven then bake for about 45-50 minutes.

Quick tip: Test the cake by inserting a toothpick. The cake is baked when the toothpick comes out clean.

9. Serve with favorite fruits or whipped cream, if desired.

NUTRITION FACTS

Serving Size: 1 (137 g)
Servings Per Recipe: 8

	Amount Per Serving	% Daily Value
Calories 295.4		
Calories from Fat 49	16%	

Amount Per Serving	% Daily Value
Total Fat 5.5g	8%
Saturated Fat 3.0g	15%
Cholesterol 18.0mg	6%
Sugars 32.5 g	
Sodium 44.5mg	1%
Total Carbohydrate 54.8g	18%
Dietary Fiber 2.7g	10%
Sugars 32.5 g	130%
Protein 6.7g	13%

Ice Cream Sundae Cupcakes

Prep Time: 15 mins

Total Time: 35 mins

Serves: 5-7, **Yield:** 10 cupcakes

Ingredients

- 10 chocolate cupcakes
- 1 pint vanilla ice cream
- 1 batch whipped cream frosting
- 1 package gluten-free candy sprinkles
- 10 frozen cherries

Directions

1. Place your favorite cupcakes on a platter or tray.
2. Top the cupcakes with scooped ice cream.
3. Frost whipped cream on top of the ice cream.
4. Dust gluten-free candy sprinkles on top.
5. Finish off with a cherry then serve immediately.

NUTRITION FACTS

Serving Size: 1 (37 g)
Servings Per Recipe: 5

Amount Per Serving	% Daily Value
Calories 114.8	
Calories from Fat 56	49%

Amount Per Serving	% Daily Value
Total Fat 6.2g	9%
Saturated Fat 3.8g	19%
Cholesterol 25.1mg	8%
Sugars 12.1 g	
Sodium 45.7mg	1%
Total Carbohydrate 13.4g	4%
Dietary Fiber 0.4g	1%
Sugars 12.1 g	48%
Protein 2.0g	4%

Banana Cupcakes With Peanut Butter Buttercream

Prep Time: 20 mins

Total Time: 43 mins

Serves: 12

Ingredients

Cupcakes

- 1 1/4 cups all-purpose gluten-free flour
- 1 teaspoon baking powder
- 1 teaspoon xanthan gum
- 3/4 teaspoon baking soda
- 1/4 teaspoon salt
- 2 large very ripe bananas, plus
- 1 yellow banana (peeled and smashed)
- 1/2 cup plain low-fat Greek yogurt
- 1 1/2 teaspoons vanilla extract

- 1 cup dates, pasted (blend 1 cup of pitted dates and 1/2-1 cup of hot water until smooth)
- 2 tablespoons grade b dark maple syrup
- 1/4 cup unsalted butter, room temperature
- 1 large egg
- 1 large egg yolk

Frosting
- 1 1/2 cups powdered sugar
- 1 tablespoon vanilla extract
- 1/4 cup unsalted butter, room temperature
- 1/2 cup natural-style peanut butter (use smooth but do not use old-fashioned or freshly ground)

Directions
1. For the Cupcakes
2. Preheat the oven to 350°F temperature.
3. Use paper liners to line 12 standard muffin cups.
4. In a small bowl, put in the smashed bananas then pour the vanilla and sour cream. Mix well then set aside.
5. In medium bowl, mix the date paste and butter until creamy. Pour and mix the maple syrup then add the egg yolk and egg. Beat well then set aside.
6. In another small bowl, sieve the flour, salt, xanthan gum, baking soda and baking powder.
7. Pour 1/3 of the banana mixture then half of the flour mixture into the medium bowl then mix well.
8. Pour and mix the 2/3 of the banana mixture and the remaining half of the flour mixture.
9. Finally pour the remaining 3/3 of the banana mixture then mix well.
10. Pour 1/4 cup of batter into each muffin cups.
11. Place the muffin cups into the preheated oven then bake for about 20-23 minutes. Quick tip: Test the muffin by inserting a toothpick. The muffin is baked when the toothpick comes out clean.
12. Take out and move the muffins into a wire rack then cool completely.

For the frosting
1. Beat the peanut butter and butter in a small bowl until smooth.
2. Add and mix the vanilla.
3. Gradually pour and mix the powdered sugar until the desired consistency is achieved.
4. Add a bit of 2% milk if desired then mix to smooth again.
5. Frost on top of the muffins to serve.

NUTRITION FACTS

Serving Size: 1 (101 g)
Servings Per Recipe: 12

Amount Per Serving	% Daily Value
Calories 283.4	
Calories from Fat 127	45%

Amount Per Serving	% Daily Value
Total Fat 14.1g	21%
Saturated Fat 6.3g	31%
Cholesterol 51.8mg	17%
Sugars 30.3 g	
Sodium 175.5mg	7%
Total Carbohydrate 37.0g	12%
Dietary Fiber 2.4g	9%
Sugars 30.3 g	121%
Protein 4.7g	9%

Jelly Donut Cupcakes

Prep Time: 15 mins

Total Time: 35 mins

Serves: 4-6, **Yield:** 10 cupcakes (about)

Ingredients

For the cupcakes
- 3 eggs
- 1/2 cup applesauce
- 1/2 cup grapeseed oil
- 1/2 cup agave nectar
- 1 tablespoon vanilla extract
- 1/2 cup coconut flour
- 1/2 teaspoon celtic sea salt
- 1/4 teaspoon baking soda

For the filling
- 1/2 cup raspberry jam
- 1 tablespoon arrowroot

For the topping
- 2 tablespoons xylitol sugar

Directions
1. For the cupcakes
2. Preheat the oven to 350°F temperature.
3. Use a food processor to mix the eggs, vanilla, agave, grapeseed oil and apple sauce.
4. Add and mix the baking soda, salt and coconut flour then set aside to thicken a bit.
5. Spoon 2 tablespoonfuls of the batter into the cupcake tins.
6. Top the batter with one teaspoonful of raspberry filling.
7. Top with another tablespoonful of batter to cover the filling.
8. Place the cupcakes tins into the preheated oven then bake for about 20-25 minutes.
9. Take out the cupcakes then cool for about 20 minutes.
10. Slightly top each cupcake with xylitol sugar. Cool then serve.

For the filling
1. In a small bowl, stir the arrowroot powder and raspberry jam well.
2. Use unbleached paper liners to line the cupcake tins.

NUTRITION FACTS

Serving Size: 1 (99 g)
Servings Per Recipe: 4

Amount Per Serving	% Daily Value
Calories 472.3	
Calories from Fat 279	59%

Amount Per Serving	% Daily Value
Total Fat 31.0g	47%
Saturated Fat 3.7g	18%
Cholesterol 158.6mg	52%
Sugars 26.3 g	
Sodium 443.9mg	18%
Total Carbohydrate 42.6g	14%
Dietary Fiber 0.8g	3%
Sugars 26.3 g	105%
Protein 4.9g	9%

Banana Cream Pie Cupcakes

Prep Time: 5 mins

Total Time: 20 mins

Serves: 4-6, **Yield:** 8 cupcakes

Ingredients

- 1 1/2 cups blanched almond flour
- 1 tablespoon arrowroot
- 1/4 teaspoon celtic sea salt
- 1/4 teaspoon baking soda
- 2 eggs
- 1/4 cup grapeseed oil
- 1/4 cup agave nectar
- 1 -2 very ripe banana (about 3/4 to 1 cup mashed)

Directions

1. Preheat the oven to 350°F temperature.
2. Line the cupcake tins with paper liners.

3. Mix the almond flour, baking soda, salt and arrowroot powder in a large mixing bowl.

4. Mix the eggs, agave and grapeseed oil in a medium bowl. Add and stir the mashed bananas.

5. Pour the banana mixture into the flour mixture then mix well.

6. Use a 1/4 measuring cup to scoop the batter into the lined cupcake tins.

7. Place the cupcake tins into the preheated oven then bake for about 15-18 minutes.

8. Take out the cupcakes from the oven then let it cool down.

9. Top with whipped cream frosting then serve.

NUTRITION FACTS

Serving Size: 1 (47 g)
Servings Per Recipe: 4

Amount Per Serving	% Daily Value
Calories 190.5	
Calories from Fat 145	76%

Amount Per Serving	% Daily Value
Total Fat 16.2g	24%
Saturated Fat 2.1g	10%
Cholesterol 105.7mg	35%
Sugars 3.8 g	
Sodium 259.3mg	10%
Total Carbohydrate 8.6g	2%
Dietary Fiber 0.8g	3%
Sugars 3.8 g	15%
Protein 3.4g	6%

In Closing

I love to cook. I believe it brings together families and friends. So I hope you and your family enjoy the delicious recipes in this book. And remember to save a seat for me at the table!

- Pamela

Printed in Great Britain
by Amazon

33393098R00040